The
Narrow
Foothold

Carina Birman

A
WALTER BENJAMIN
FILÒSOF ALEMANY
BERLIN 1892 PORTBOU 1940

PORTBOU 1979

Carina Birman, New York, 1950   Photo: Rose Nicolaier

THE
NARROW
FOOTHOLD

CARINA BIRMAN

"How this work was written: rung by rung, according as chance would offer a narrow foothold, and always like someone who scales dangerous heights and never allows himself a moment to look round, for fear of becoming dizzy (but also because he would save for the end the full force of the panorama opening out to him)."

Walter Benjamin, *The Arcades Project*, p.460 (English edition published by Harvard University Press, 1999).

Hearing Eye

Published by Hearing Eye 2006

Hearing Eye
Box 1, 99 Torriano Avenue
London, NW5 2RX, UK
Email:hearing_eye@torriano.org
www.hearingeye.org

ISBN 1 905082 10 X

Acknowledgements

Copies of the unedited typescript of Exodus (The Narrow Foothold) by Carina Birman
were deposited in 2005 with the Institute of Germanic Studies in the University of
London. The publishers are grateful to Astrid Schmetterling for pointing out the
significance of the manuscript and to Olwyn Hughes for recommending publication, to
Professor Howard Caygill for encouragement and providing the historical background
and introduction, to the poet Les Murray, who undertook the editing of the Germanic
English texts and to the poet Stephen Watts, for permission to reproduce his poem
'Marginal Note in Time of War'
(In the Company of Poets, Hearing Eye 2003).

The photographs of Port Bou were taken by Christopher North in January 2005
and the photographs from the family archive have been provided by
Kathy Duggan, granddaughter of Sophie Lippmann.

A CIP catalogue record for this book is available from the British Library.

Design by Kevin Fernandes
Printed in Great Britain by Aldgate Press, London E1 7RQ

Contents

Illustrations

✦ archive photographs
◇ photographs by Christopher North

Note from the publisher

On page 30 is the route taken by the refugees across the Pyrenees in the Autumn of 1940 from France to Spain. It is very difficult terrain. I accompanied Kathy Duggan and the photographer Christopher North to Port Bou to see for myself the difficulties the refugees faced in crossing the border. My first impression of Port Bou was its smell of freedom, its friendly inhabitants. Even as a young man, I was surrounded by people who wanted to survive and tried to oppose dictatorship. I would therefore have given Walter Benjamin the same advice as did Carina Birman.   **John Rety**

John Rety at the frontier overlooking Port Bou

Introduction

The author of this memoir of escape from Nazi-occupied Europe was Carina Birman (1895-1996), the Conseil Juridique at the Austrian embassy in Paris between 1926 and 1938. It tells of her escape in 1940 from Paris with her friend Sophie Lippmann (1885-1975) and their flight over the Pyrenees through Spain and Portugal to New York. Having secured a number of Mexican visas for refugee intellectuals in order to attend an arts festival, she spent a year in Mexico before moving back to New York in 1942. She subsequently pursued a distinguished legal career in the United States.

The memoir is fascinating, not only as a testimony of escape, but also as an account of the last day of the life of the celebrated philosopher and literary critic Walter Benjamin. It provides additional corroborative detail of the circumstances surrounding Benjamin's last journey as well as his state of mind during the last night of his life. It shows the desperate plight of the refugees, the corruption of Spanish border officials, as well as providing fresh information on the suicide of Walter Benjamin.

The memoir was written in 1975, but never published during the author's lifetime. The typescript was given by the author to Barbara Friedlander, the daughter of Sophie Lippmann, in 1976 and is here published for the first time.

Kathy Duggan
Howard Caygill

The Narrow Foothold

From all sides I was pressed hard to set a date for our departure. I knew I had to do it, yet inwardly I was not yet prepared to abandon a country to which I had come by my own free will, where I had lived for many years, where I felt at home and had passed the best and happiest years of my life. I was one of the very few who was not a refugee, but felt very close to this country and was deeply affected by its disastrous misfortune, more so than all those who surrounded me.

Although nobody openly announced his real departure date, it was, if not known, still felt in advance. First the Werfels were gone, then Prof. Paul Stefan, then Mrs. Zweig with her two daughters and their husbands, one of them carrying Shooshoo. What dispositions they had prepared in advance remained everyone's secret. But all had to cross the Pyrenees. They had either connections with Spanish Catholic institutions or were rich enough to order, for a lot of money, a vehicle and porters from Spain. Those for whom neither possibility was open had to walk. At that time trains were not passing the border. It was the only exit from France, all ports and other borders out to the free Atlantic being blocked.

One afternoon a few people arrived in Marseilles from the North and brought the latest news to us. They also told us that they had travelled with Nazi police in their compartment and had seen a list of names the police were looking for in the South of France. One name nearly topping the list was my own. I was warned to disappear.

This triggered the long awaited decision. Sophie was agreeable that we leave immediately. I called my sister Dele and our friend, Grete Freund, who had joined us for better or worse, and we took the train the same evening towards the nearest point on the Spanish border, via Perpignan - Banyuls - Port Bou. Everything had to be done clandestinely, to escape notice. From 8 p.m. on there was a curfew, even on the railways. At Perpignan we had to change trains, with no guides and no flashlights turned on, to find the right train for Banyuls out of many trains coming from various directions was quite a good piece of work. Yet our wandering over the tracks had brought upon us an immediate police inspection as soon as we were installed in the new train. We did not show our Mexican papers, but claimed only to be on our way to visit family in Banyuls, some kilometers away from the frontier station at Port Bou. They soon left us, cursing and swearing about the untimely disturbance.

In marvellous southern sunshine we arrived the next morning in Banyuls, where we had to investigate how to go on, get over the border and avoid all border controls. Sleeping quarters for one or two nights were easily found. By chance in Banyuls we met some Austrian socialists whom we knew from Montauban and who were usually well informed about possible ways to proceed without great danger.

As I saw some of them enter the Mayor's office, I also went in and asked for a responsible person to direct us across the mountains to Spain. The man to whom I spoke seemed to be trustworthy. I asked for his discretion and told him that we were refugees who wished to flee from France without an exit permit. He indicated to me someone who was very familiar with all the smugglers' paths, who knew the country inside out and could direct us properly. But we had to take a trial walk up the mountains with him, about two hours of climbing. I was ready to do it, my friend Grete Freund was willing to accompany me. The two others, Sophie and Dele, had to await our return.

When we arrived at a certain height we saw a deep valley before us surrounded by ranges of mountains. Our guide pointed out a particular direction and stressed that on the top of that summit there was a big, heavy square cross, which we should use as a landmark and toward which we should direct our path. That was the Spanish border. Once arrived there we should immediately ask for the nearest Spanish customs office; an immigration place. If we missed such a convenient customs office, the Spaniards might well arrest us as illegal entrants. Then he brought us back to Banyuls.

As this excursion was not a tiring one, we decided to leave the following morning. The landlady prepared us hot coffee and at 4 a.m. we started our ascent together with the wine-growers, as it was vintage day, and thus we would not attract special attention.

We walked through vineyards where the famous Banyuls grapes were growing; these were to be used in the famous sweet dessert wine, the best France produces. We were only passing by and had little time to enjoy the delicacy which surrounded us in abundance. We were directed towards the top of the rock on which we were climbing. This took us incredibly longer than the day before. Other small groups of refugees passed us, marching in the same direction as we. We could not start conversations with peasants near us, the more so as they were not prepared to talk to us.

When we finally arrived at the summit we had been shown, we saw the valley before us, at the foot of the mountain ranges. Now we had to look for the cross, to find our direction. We looked and saw a cross on a mountain top, then turning around we saw another summit with a cross. In all directions there were crosses on the mountains. We made out four summits, each with a similar cross at a similar altitude. What to do? We sat down, searching our make-shift maps to learn what direction to choose.

In the meantime we were joined by an elderly gentleman, a younger female and her son. The gentleman, a German university professor named Walter Benjamin, was on the point of having a heart attack. The strain of mountain climbing on an extremely hot September day, together with the anxious endeavour to escape German arrest was too much for him. As we were at a resting place, we ran in all directions in search of some water to help the sick man. Slowly he recovered and we continued our wandering; the new arrivals in our vicinity had to be ready to help if necessary.

We wandered about here and there and at sunset we met our first Spaniards on the other side of the mountain. Sophie was completely exhausted and asked where she could get some water. A man disappeared and after a few moments brought a glass of water. Overjoyed by this help we gave him a few coins which we had ready. The water refreshed Sophie and we were able to continue our search. We saw what we thought to be our first Spanish customs office, which we had been told to enter. To our dismay we learned it was the second one, and the police captain in charge there declared us under arrest and obliged to return to the French border. As he was adamant, I asked as a favour to pass the night in a quiet place, and promised that we would return the following morning.

My promise covered myself, Sophie, my sister Dele and my friend Grete Freund: it did not include Prof. Benjamin and his companion who had a young son, although I had also presented their papers at their suggestion. He did not utter a word. When this request of mine was granted I was told that the next morning at 10 a.m. Spanish police would pick us up and take us back to the French border. We shivered, but could not say anything. At the same time my neck was seized by a big male hand; I was turned around and commanded by a stocky man to order my party to follow him closely. We were to be accommodated overnight in a special police hotel. We were divided into four little groups; Prof. Benjamin alone received a room for himself: his companion with son another place, Sophie and I a room and my sister and Grete Freund a small cell. We gathered to discuss how to proceed to avoid the dreaded return to the border. We knew that the border police were not only linked with the Nazi Secret Service, but nearly all of them were Nazi informers and acting upon Nazi orders. They all had the lists of persons wanted by the Germans. Our return would have been the end of our freedom and would have meant certain deportation.

In addition to a small amount of regular currency banknotes, Sophie and I also had a few gold coins with us. Sophie, based on her knowledge acquired from her literary upbringing, was sure that bribing the Spaniards with such gold coins would make them more amenable and helpful. During the dark hours of the night she prowled about to find the hotel warden and tell him of our predicament so as to enlist him to help us with the police. In case of success he, as well as the police captain, would get from us all the gold coins we had. She was not afraid he might murder us on the spot to get hold of the promised loot. She trusted her ability to tell the character of a person from facial features and considered this gate watcher was not a murderer, merely extremely greedy, a very risky judgment in this instance.

He promised to put her in contact with the police at sunrise, although he was sure that only the captain could annul an order he himself had issued, and he was not available before 10 a.m.

On her search for the hotel man she heard in the hallway loud rattling from one of the neighbouring rooms. She returned and asked me to look into this situation. I entered the room and found Prof. Benjamin in a desolate state of mind and in a completely exhausted physical condition. He told me that by no means was he willing to return to the border, or to move out of this hotel. When I remarked that there was no alternative than to leave, he declared that there was one for him. He hinted that he had some very effective poisonous pills with him. He was lying half naked in his bed and had his very beautiful big golden grandfather watch with open cover on a little board near him, observing the time constantly.

I told him of our attempted gold bribery and implored him to abandon the idea of suicide, or at least to await the result of Sophie's dealings with the local authorities, about which he was very pessimistic. I left him only when his lady companion came in and kept guard with him. I did not know him at all, and was thus unaware whether it was the right thing to do to hinder him from departing this life, which he seemed to abhor. The next morning we heard that he had succeeded and was no more amongst us.

All through the early hours the telephone was in action. All kinds of personalities were reached and asked for assistance. In the meantime the warden gave us a hot coffee. We had not finished swallowing it when two uniformed Spanish gendarmes appeared at the entrance, claiming us and our miserable belongings.

I told them that somebody had intervened for us and that we were to get Spanish entry papers at any minute. We were waiting for them right now. They gave us half an hour, then they took over the telephone. While the police captain was never available to us, they got through to him in a couple of seconds. Thereupon they insisted that we leave with them and go with them to the summit of the mountains, to the first point of entry on Spanish soil. There, and only there, our entrance permits were awaiting us. So, we had to go, crossing the village of Port Bou, flanked by the two gendarmes, who played gentleman executioner by carrying our rucksacks. The ascent of the mountain, which took us a couple of hours, was less painful because at the end of this Calvary we saw the mirage of entrance permits.

On the summit the gendarmes placed us in front of a thick rope, the border between Spain and France. We saw French and Nazi officers on the other side. But we saw no hut or office where we could have obtained our entrance permits. Only a telephone booth. We protested vehemently to the gendarmes, accusing them of luring us under false pretences to the lion's den and playing a trick on us. They suggested that we phone the Spanish police at Port Bou claiming the entrance permits; they even gave us some coins for the telephone. We were told we were too impatient and that at a later hour we might expect to receive these permits. We were desperate. The gendarmes laughingly said how grateful we should be to them that they did not untie the rope and, as they were advised to do, hand us literally over to the custom officers on the other side of the border. With that pronouncement they disappeared and left us at the mercy of the unknown.

There we were sitting on rocks and burnt out slopes. We were so depressed that we did not even notice that the sky was becoming darker and darker, although it was early in the afternoon. A thunderstorm! No, a rainstorm, heavy masses of water were soon pouring over us. No shelter anywhere, desert like surroundings. If we would not make a decision soon we would be washed away without mercy, maybe in different directions. We weighed our possibilities. There was only one direction with uncertain issue, all the others meant death. So we decided to return to Spain. There was no hope of walking down. There were no passable tracks any more, one could only sit on stones and try to glide down. We knew we would tear our only dress, our only pair of stockings, but better nothing than being exposed to these calamities on the mountain tops as the rain became heavier by the minute.

Between 5-6 p.m. we arrived at the bottom of the mountain, where we looked and asked for the nearest Spanish customs office. We were warned not to insist on going there, as hours before two groups of refugees had been arrested and delivered to the Germans. The people took us for gypsies; our rain drenched appearance made us unrecognisable. But here too we had no alternative, we had to go.

We approached the customs office and were first chased away as gypsies, but upon my insistence, a loud controversy followed, until the head of the office appeared. Who was he? The Police captain, unattainable for us in the morning.

He approached us by saying that these were familiar voices, he had heard them before. His staff had explained to him that we were gypsies, who were not entitled to approach the office. He looked at us, recognised us and asked me for the papers of all of us. I gave them to him, asking once more for the promised entrance permits. Without a word he disappeared, but soon came back with a stack of chairs in his arms. To each of us he gave a chair to rest on while he again disappeared with our papers. We were sure that we had given away our last important belongings, our travelling papers. We did not expect to see them again.

He left us there quite some time, then he appeared suddenly with a very morose look, approached me and pushed something into one of the pockets of my raincoat. Then he said in his best French. "I have visaed your 'papels' (papers) and marked out a special route to follow via Spain and a special exit place where you have to follow if you do not want to be harmed in this country. Besides you have to leave Port Bou this very night." We did not believe our ears. Here was another miracle!

We were now directed to the customs inspection. Sophie, my sister Dele and Grete Freund passed it easily. I, however, was kept back because the officials had found in my purse 200 French francs, which I had omitted to declare. In all the excitement I had forgotten them. It took quite some time until I could convince the custom people of my involuntary error by abandoning this amount to them. As soon as we were officially permitted on Spanish soil, yesterday's hotel keeper took hold of me, took me aside, pushed me away from the others and asked for the gold coins. How much we had, where we kept them? We had to give them all to him as previously promised by Sophie during the night. As the speaker of the group he addressed himself solely to me. So it seems that she was right. Her offer had worked, even in our absence. He must have communicated with the police captain to rescind his previous order, but too late to retain us. He must have prayed the whole day for heavenly inspiration on our part to find our way back to his office. Otherwise the amazingly prompt recognition of our voices by the Police captain would have been unlikely.

We had, Sophie and I, already determined during the night how many gold coins of our small hidden treasure should be offered, in case we got a positive response to our request for admission, and we had set apart the bail. I kept it, while Sophie who had better hiding places in her wardrobe than I, took the rest.

Now, Sophie had already passed the inspection, no money search, her reserve was safe; so I showed all my pockets, my handbag and extracted slowly a little paper packet with the gold coins. I felt I was being watched from afar, by the captain who ostensibly continued his regular official functions. My hotel warden stood in front of me very tense, getting bigger and bigger eyes until he got hold of the coins, then he relaxed. I rearranged my various pockets and bags and raised my head. Another person looked at me with friendly eyes. A metamorphosis! A kind, human, compassionate person was at my side. He promised to take care of everything: he urged me to have confidence in him and to exhort the others of my group to do likewise.

An amiable nod by the police captain, and we were dismissed. The hotel keeper brought us back to his regular inn, which was last night's police shelter, assigned large airy rooms to all of us and instructed us to appear, in an hour's time, in the big dining room for supper.

We were completely drenched by the rain. The excitement and the unnatural humid weather had let us forget it for a short while, but now we asked only for hot tea for our refreshment. We did not dare to ask for more, although we were very hungry, as Spain was known to be suffering a serious famine, with scarcity of nearly all sorts of food, and we did not intend to provoke some altercation about it. Besides, we had just come down from France which had started to suffer serious shortages of foodstuffs of all kinds, no butter, no milk, no eggs, no bread, very little cheese, etc. We were asked to be patient and to leave to our host what he would offer us.

When we entered the dining room a little later we were confronted by so lavish a banquet table with food so plentiful, so variegated, so rich, prepared in different ways, butter, bread, chicken, toast, magnificent Spanish wine on the table, that we were completely confused. The setting was spotless, crystal, elegant china, silver everywhere. It was all on the house, said our innkeeper, to alleviate our uneasiness!

We had, however, not yet started the meal, when the light was turned off and there entered a Catholic priest at the head of a procession of about twenty monks in black and white robes, each carrying a lit candle, singing a religious litany, crossing our dining room and mounting to the upper floor.

We were told that they had come from a neighbouring monastery to say a requiem at the death-bed of Prof. Benjamin and to bury him. We had quite forgotten this most unfortunate occurrence during last night, and although we knew Mr. Benjamin to have been Jewish, we made no remark and left this declaration to his lady companion. She never said anything of the kind and let them take the body of the defunct.

Before we withdrew to our rooms, the hotel keeper promised to wake us up in time to catch the night train for Barcelona, which we were ordered by the Police captain to take. He also took all our clothes and underwear, heated his stoves and furnaces and had them completely dried before we had to put them on again.

We were up before the awakener knocked on our doors and brought us our clothes. To our surprise Sophie found in her bed a broken glass frame with a big photo of her late husband. Where she had hidden and carried it before, how it came into her bed, I do not know, and she never explained it to me. But instead of being unhappy about this broken keepsake, she abandoned herself to a superstitious impulse, laughed, was very happy and saw in it a positive sign for the outcome of our further adventures.

Outside was a racing furious thunderstorm, yesterday's rain had not stopped. The hotel keeper had umbrellas for all of us, brought us to the railway station, not far away, bought the tickets for us to Barcelona and put us in the right train.

Adieu, charmant pays de France!

Adieu, Port Bou.

The compartments of the train were typical European ones, small; narrow with windows and glass doors and a glazed corridor as a passageway. While we were discussing our further itineraries, a man passed back and forth in front of our door for quite a while. When the train started to roll, he entered our compartment; we thought it was a ticket controller. Instead of tickets he asked us about our destination, our plans, and our preparedness for events to be faced. Great astonishment on our part. He then said he had seen us two days before, arriving at the foot of the mountains and asking him for water for a person completely exhausted. He said we gave him an abundant tip for his natural charitable gesture, although he had seen that we were fleeing France and were poor. He now wished to reciprocate this good deed of ours as well as he could. He advised us to ask for a specific porter at the station in Barcelona in case we needed advice or directions. Also he wanted to know whether we had personal snapshots, such as passport photos. We had plenty. He then instructed us to go with these photos to a particular workers' office and ask to be issued with a Spanish identification card (*tarjeta de identificación*) and after we received these cards to go to the ticket office and purchase our tickets to Madrid and on to Badajoz, the exit from Spain. We should pay the lowest fare for a first class ticket.

Our first trip in Barcelona was to that office for a Spanish *tarjeta de identificación*. I fell when crossing the rails and hurt myself so badly that I could scarcely move. No hope of my continuing on to that office. My companions intended to go all the same and would try to secure me my card too. They were lucky and got what they wanted. I was waiting in a nearby coffee shop, eating an apple for breakfast, one which I had taken with me from our last night's dinner. No sooner did I bite into the apple than it was snatched out of my mouth by a tiny Spanish youngster who ran away as if he had stolen a treasure. For him it was a treasure; he looked as if he were half starved. At the same time I was surrounded by about a dozen children, all so-called shoe-shine boys, and a category I saw for the first time. They yelled to me in English "Shoeshine, shoeshine". I let them clean my abominably dirty shoes and gave them a few small coins for the work, which satisfied them completely. Then I had the shoes of all my companions shined.

My companions inquired about our train to Madrid and the connection to the border. We had only one the next morning, so they bought the tickets. We were warned that there were Nazi Secret Police (SS) everywhere and that we were constantly observed. So we took the first train available to Madrid the same afternoon. Madrid made a terrible impression on us, a city half destroyed by the Civil War. Hardly anything to eat and begging children constantly assailing us. Yet we had to take a room in a hotel not far from the station. Although entire districts there were destroyed and unusable for pedestrians, we wished to have a glance at the city, its lay-out, its palaces. We took a cab, as I could not walk, and made the tour of this metropolis of the South. We also went into the Prado, to get an impression of its magnificent treasures. This was the one luxury on our flight.

Then, observed, surrounded, followed by Secret Service Police, we finally arrived at the railway station to take the train to Badajoz, the Spanish-Portuguese border town where we had to change trains: the Spanish ones could not pass out of their country, as they have a different gauge from the other European rail systems.

Badajoz is a city built fortresslike, full of medieval romance where you might expect to meet Don Quixote or Sancho Panza turning around the corner. But the atmosphere was still full of anxiety. After having passed the custom control without any difficulties, we bought tickets to Lisbon at the Portuguese ticket office of Elvas, the Portuguese railway station at the border on our route to Lisbon, and boarded the train.

We were now out of danger in a boundless free universe, a neutral country. Safe! We could breathe again at ease. Suddenly, after a few minutes travel, the train entered a railway station the like I have never seen before. It looked like a tremendous fair, where all kinds of food never seen before or not encountered for a long time was leisurely exposed, long sausages, smoked meat hanging from the ceiling, fruits from Africa and the tropical colonies of Portugal lying everywhere. We could touch it from the window of our train and buy whatever we wished at incredibly low prices. It seemed to us unreal that a few minutes away from a country stricken by a severe famine we could ride through a paradise like this.

After a short halt to let all passengers enjoy the surprising plenty, the train continued on its route. The scenery was now quite different. Vast, flat plains, brilliant sunshine and glittering walls reflecting the sun's rays to blind us. In order to resist the burning heat of the sun the houses were walled not with bricks but with glazed tiles, so that the landlords were at no expense for repairing walls. The Government took care that the buildings did not make a decrepit impression, fining those house-owners who neglected their upkeep. It was late in the evening when we arrived in Lisbon.

For the first time Sophie and I had difficulties in making ourselves understood. We were looking for a small, not too expensive hotel, if possible not far from the centre of the city. We explained it to a taxi driver who drove us endlessly through the city, through dark streets and alleys, until he stopped at a place where he seemed to know the owner. We were completely ignored: he talked with the female in charge who could explain how much to pay for the fare.

Then she took charge of us. The premises made a strange impression. The rooms were elaborately furnished in red plush, the windows closed, shades down, curtains drawn; the air was hot and heavy. When we showed unhappiness at these surroundings, the woman in charge disappeared and came back with enormous bottles of perfume spray which she dispensed so generously that we nearly fainted. We gave up; we were too tired. Knowing that we were staying in a classically set up brothel, we hated to lie down on the beds. But we were overcome with fatigue and slept until the next morning. We left our belongings there and tried to get to the centre of the city, to the great hotels where we expected to find Mrs. Zweig and her children. We did see her and the porter of her hotel was able to book rooms for us in a neighboring reputable boarding house on the Praça Restauradores. No difficulty with the Madame; we left the brothel, to her regret.

Here we felt ground again. Sophie had not heard from her daughter and sisters in London since the fall of France. I bought a Portuguese newspaper and read the headlines, "Blitz over London". Already when leaving Marseilles I had seen in the papers that Hitler had ordered the Luftwaffe to bomb London and southern England as intensely as possible. I did not dare draw Sophie's attention to this at the time, to avoid exciting her needlessly, since it was impossible for us to do anything about it, but now I could not hold back any more. Sophie took it in her stride and although constantly worried she never annoyed her companions with her personal plight.

We went to the Post Office where we hoped to have some mail as we had advised London and Sophie's daughter-in-law Alisa Lippmann in New York of our projected flight to Portugal. We did not know whether her son, Dr. Heinz Lippmann, was still in London or had already joined his wife and daughter in New York. We had a short note from Heinz in New York where he gave his mother the name and address of a friend of his, a Mr. Terlo of Lisbon, a Sephardic Jew, who certainly would be helpful to relatives and friends of Heinz, if they should need assistance there.

It was October 1st when we arrived in Lisbon. The imminent Jewish Yom Kippur was 'before the door'. We did not know how to move around inexpensively within the city: we looked for neighbourhood places to visit and this way we found the big Sephardic synagogue, not far from our boarding house. At noon on Yom Kippur we went there, showed the Shammes a paper with the the name of Mr. Terlo and asked to see him. He brought him out into the wonderful garden of that house of God. We explained our plight to him and from that time on and until our departure he was our guardian angel.

Through him we learned that there was no direct boat from Portugal to Mexico and that we had to pass through the United States in transit. This meant another visa that we had to solicit from unfriendly Foreign Service American Consuls, who were more anti-semitically inclined than any other group of diplomatic officials. And how to get our boat tickets? Our money was nearly all used up.

The International Police Control Service in Lisbon granted us only a stay of 10-15 days. When I enquired about the papers to be submitted to the American Consul I was told that to obtain the transit visa I had to show that I am Jewish. Sophie had her regular birth certificate showing that her parents were Jews, but I had only a recent copy of my birth certificate and nowhere was there the mention that I was the daughter of Jewish parents. The heading "Israelitische Kulturgemeinde" (Community of Israelitic Culture) was not enough. So with Mr. Terlo's help, a Lisbon Jewish rabbi issued a certificate to me that I was Jewish.

We also had to approach a Jewish refugee committee which tried to advance money for the boat tickets to the neediest, and to convince them that we had to have the money for the passage, the more so as the Portuguese authorities were harassing us constantly for an early departure. Sophie, as a German refugee, had no great difficulty in convincing them, while I, until then a non-refugee, and what was most suspicious for them, a sort of official of the Legation of a country, Austria, which had the reputation of being very anti-semitic, must be a hidden "goyte", now trying to take advantage of their services. I had to cable to New York, to one of the heads of a Literary Refugee Committee whom I knew, and ask them to confirm their knowledge of my real Jewish descent; this helped.

We were promised the ticket by the Jewish Committee. Mr. Terlo helped us to get reservations on a Portuguese boat, the Nyassa, which was to leave Lisbon about the 23rd of November.

Mrs. Zweig, her children and my friend Grete Freund had left already before us on a better boat than ours.

The only obstacle now was the American Consul, who when I saw him personally promised me to grant us two weeks stay in the U.S.A. on a transit visa. When I got our passports back they were stamped 24 hours stay only in the United States. When I admonished the Consul for his broken word he threatened to tear off the visa if I continued to object.

My sister Dele became independent in Lisbon. She had found there an immigration visa from our brother Hans Birman for Brazil and intended to use it. The Brazilian visa was easily obtainable for her. My friend Grete Freund also found other ways and got a visitor's visa to New York. The two Mexican immigration visas became obsolete for them.

I had, like my sister Dele, found on my arrival in Lisbon an immigration visa for Brazil, procured by my brother Hans, who was a permanent resident there working successfully on his own as a construction engineer, but I wished to proceed to Mexico and make use of the generous attitude of the Mexican government.

When we were leaving for the U.S.A., however, I had to leave my sister Dele in Lisbon as she was only booked for a passage some time later. She then went to Brazil and is still living there.

Our boat was overcrowded; it was our first big voyage across the ocean. We were six persons in a very small space, but luckily we had a bedstead. Many refugees were lying on the floor.

The boat moved slowly, very slowly. The food never arrived other than ice cold on our plates. There were roaches in the washrooms, sometimes no electric current and no heat whatsoever in the late fall; we were shivering day and night.

The officers were anxious not to meet German U-boats, so were we, as an examination of papers and a selection of passengers to be taken off was unavoidable. The Germans really did not respect ships under neutral flags.

Then, one day, suddenly I noticed that the boat had stopped moving. We had come to a complete standstill. When I questioned the ship's officers they denied it in order to avoid panic amongst the passengers, but I was sure that the motors did not work. Only after several days was a slow, very slow movement to be felt, and slowly this 50-year-old former German coastal schooner began advancing again.

On December 4th 1940, at 5 a.m. we saw the Statue of Liberty, and slowly yet majestically the Nyassa entered New York harbour. We were all on deck with tears of emotion in our eyes.

Scientist Suicide in Spain

Many Refugees Believed Victims of Mountain Gangs

LISBON, Oct. 7 (ONA.) — The suicide of Prof. *Walter Benjamin,* a well-known psychologist, and the mysterious disappearance of many refugees in the mountainous Franco-Spanish frontier zone were reported by reliable sources here today.

The professor, during recent years attached to the faculty of the Sorbonne at Paris and to the Institute for Social Research at N. Y. Columbia University, committed suicide by poison at the Franco-Spanish frontier town of Port-Bou after Spanish authorities forbade him to continue his projected journey to Lisbon and the United States, according to four women friends who said they witnessed his death.

At the same time it was reported that many refugees who succeeded in getting into Spain from France had disappeared without trace during recent weeks. It was feared here that they had been killed in the mountainous frontier area by gangs of bandits who had promised to smuggle them across the border.

Prof. Benjamin, who had been granted a visa by the United States but had not been granted an exit permit by the French authorities, succeeded in slipping across the border.

The Spanish police chief at Port Bou, however, took them sternly to task for their getaway over the border and told them he would not permit them to continue their journey. The refugees asked for permission to rest a couple of hours and discuss their next move, a request which was granted. During this period of waiting, the professor, despairing of completing his journey, took a strong dose of poison from a phial he carried and died before the horrified eyes of his four women companions.

The professor was buried in the Catholic cemetery at Port Bou, although he was a Jew, because officials found on his person a note from a prominent French Catholic clergyman to Spanish Catholic church notables urging them to help the professor complete his trip.

First mention of Benjamin's suicide in the New York weekly, *Aufbau*, 11 October 1940.

Marginal note in time of war
Poem by Stephen Watts

His name was not written — Hannah Arendt

Walter Benjamin took his own
life out of pure exhaustion, walking
into the mountains against love's gravity
up the scarp slope of his melting reason
to where he was abandoned by language.
Huge lethargies in the world glutted him
then stiff blood came, pulsed out in coils.
Who knows where he could have gone to
after that, except he couldn't go on, burst
by the butchered choice of angel history,
a tremendous shattering tossed across his
face, tiny maggots gobbling on sunlight,
fascisms in the honeys of his friendship.
His name unwritten, nowhere to be seen.
He who was the loveliest among people.
Why did no-one tell him when he lived?
Nothing was left to hold him on the hill.
Angels could not put back insane reason.
Exhaustion killed him, more than terror,
more than despair, or a theology of dirt.
At the end — when the angel of history
called out his name to mock him — he
walked higher up into the blind frontier
and took his own life on a hillside that
looks over the sea: one of the loveliest
places on earth, as Hannah Arendt said,
and like himself, halfway up
and halfway down.

Testimonies to a death
Howard Caygill

Until the early 1980s the main sources for information concerning the death of Walter Benjamin were a letter by Henny Gurland, one of his travelling companions across the Pyrenees, and a memoir by the political philosopher Hannah Arendt who later followed the same route out of Nazi Europe. The account of his death written by Benjamin's friend and scholar of Jewish mysticism Gershom Scholem in *Walter Benjamin: Story of a Friendship* (Faber and Faber, 1982) rests largely on Gurland's letter, which he reproduces. This is the closest historical document to the events described, and was long considered to be the only surviving testimony of Benjamin's doomed attempt to escape to Spain.

Henny Gurland's letter to a relative of her husband (Akadi) is dated October 11, 1940 and was forwarded first to Benjamin's friend and colleague the philosopher Theodor Wiesengrund Adorno at the exiled Institute for Social Research in New York and then by him to Gershom Scholem at the University of Jerusalem. Gurland wrote: 'In the meantime you must have heard about our terrible experience with Benjamin. He, José (Gurland's teenage son), and I left Marseilles together in order to share the trip. In M, I became rather good friends with him and he found me suitable as a travelling companion. On the road through the Pyrenees we met Birman, her sister [sic] Frau Lippmann, and the Freund woman from Das Tagebuch[1]. For all of us those 12 hours were an absolutely horrible ordeal.'[2] She continues 'At 7 in the morning Frau Lippmann called me down because Benjamin asked for me. He told me he had taken vast quantities of morphine at 10 the preceding evening and that I should try and present the matter as illness; he gave me a letter addressed to me and Adorno…'[3] Hannah Arendt would subsequently describe how the border officials were so moved by his suicide that they allowed the party to leave for Portugal.[4] Gurland, however, had a different recollection: 'You know Birman and judge our situation when I tell you that when she and the others arrived at the border up there, they refused to go on and said they agreed to be redirected to the detention camp in Figueras,' adding 'money changed hands, and quite a lot of it'.

Gurland's account has been largely corroborated by the emergence of subsequent testimony. Curiosity concerning the events in Port Bou on the night of September 25, 1940 was nourished by mention of a suitcase carried by Benjamin suspected to contain a lost work. Chance decreed that further testimony would emerge, even if this would not settle the fate of the legendary lost suitcase. In March 1980 Scholem received a letter from Schimon Abramsky, Professor of Jewish Studies at University College, London, describing how during a sabbatical at Stanford University he met at dinner the aunt of a colleague's wife who claimed to have crossed the Pyrenees with Benjamin. This was Lisa Fittko whom Scholem contacted in Chicago and who late in the year (November) wrote a testimony describing the passage over the mountains.

Lisa Fittko served a guide for refugees across the mountains, her account (written in English) provides valuable evidence for the journey across the mountains, even though she left the party before returning to France.[5] Her account is especially interesting for her description of her meeting of the second group of refugees who crossed the Pyrenees that day: 'Putting down on paper the details that my memory brings back about this first time I crossed the border on the route Lister, a nebulous picture surfaces from wherever it has been buried all these years. Three women - two of them I know vaguely - crossing our reading; though in a haze, I see us standing there and talking for a short while. They had come up by a different road and they continued their way down the Spanish side separately.'

One of that party, also mentioned by Gurland - Carina Birman [1975] – also wrote a memoir of this meeting and the events that preceded and followed, and this too was discovered by chance during a dinner conversation between Astrid Schmetterling of Goldsmiths College and Barbara Friedlander, Sophie Lippmann's daughter, in 1998. The memoir offers more detail of the crossing and the death of Benjamin, corroboration of Gurland and Fittko's account while adding new details to the account of events during the night of Benjamin's suicide. With it the dossier of testimony to Benjamin's death is probably as complete as it will ever be, leaving many questions still open for future discussion.

Footnotes

[1] The anti-Nazi, anti-communist fortnightly magazine, published at that time in Paris and founded in Germany by Stefan Grossman.

[2] *Walter Benjamin: History of a Friendship*, pp.224-5.

[3] Ibid.

[4] See her memoir *Walter Benjamin: 1892-1940* reprinted as the introduction to the collection of Benjamin's essays *Illuminations*.

[5] For Scholem's account see his article '*Ueber Benjamins letzte Flucht: zu einem Bericht von Lisa Fittko*' written in 1981 and published in his collection *Walter Benjamin und sein Engel*, Suhrkamp Verlag, Frankfurt am Main, 1983. Fittko's account may be found in *Walter Benjamin: Gesammelte Schriften V.2*, pp. 1183-1202, also published by Suhrkamp Verlag, Frankfurt am Main 1982. Following this lead, the German editor of Benjamin's writings Rolf Tiedemann also succeeded in locating Joseph Gurland, then a professor at Brown University, whose memories of the crossing were unfortunately but understandably obscure.

Howard Caygill is Professor of Cultural History, Goldsmiths College, University of London, and author of '*Walter Benjamin: The Colour of Experience*'.

Notes on individuals by Kathy Duggan

Barbara Friedlander

My mother Barbara (Bärbel), Sophie Lippmann's daughter, was handed this document by Carina in 1976 the year after Sophie died, and she kept it among her papers until the present publication.

In 1938, at the age of 23, Barbara left Paris where she had been studying and went to London to look after her favourite aunt, Grete, Sophie's sister. Grete had settled in England and was dying of leukaemia. This sad circumstance mercifully saved my mother from being part of the group that crossed the Pyrenees.

Heinz Lippmann

At the time of the Pyrenean crossing, Heinz Lippmann, my uncle, Sophie Lippmann's son, was already living in New York where he had re-joined his Italian wife Alisa and their baby daughter Constance. He left Genoa in 1939 just before war broke out. Due to the quota system Alisa and Constance had left for America the year before.

Sophie Lippmann

My grandmother Sophie Lippmann, née Moskiewicz, was born on the 2nd April 1885 in Breslau (now the Polish town of Wrocklav). Charming and talented, she was a celebrated beauty known in the town as "the most beautiful girl in Breslau." She was a qualified French teacher. She also wrote poetry published in German magazines and newspapers and later in the New York magazine, The Aufbau. She married Felix Lippmann, co-owner of *Gebrüder Lippmann und Cohn* textile wholesalers, in the year 1906.

Not at all religious, Sophie considered herself an 'Enlightenment' free thinker, her great heroine being the writer George Sand.

Felix and Sophie had two children, Heinz born in 1908 and my mother, Barbara (Barbel) born in 1914. They loved entertaining in their beautiful house in Gabitzstrasse designed by the architect Stahl-Urach. They counted many artists among their friends - Döblin, author of *Berlin Alexander Platz*, Nellie Sachs, the Nobel prize-winning poet, and the painter, Eugen Spiro.

In 1936 Sophie moved to Paris and lived there with her friend Carina Birman. Felix went to live in Genoa joining his two children; Heinz who was just starting a medical practice, something he had not been able to do as a Jew in Nazi Germany and Barbara who had joined her brother in 1934 after leaving school. Sadly Felix died of a stroke at the end of his first year in Italy.

Once Sophie arrived in Mexico she worked in a household and was told off for using too much scouring powder. This was not surprising as she had never set foot in the Gabitzstrasse kitchen. However, she laboured diligently and subsequently worked in a factory in New York where she became forewoman. Later she taught French again.

I remember Granny, who died in New York in 1975, as a very grand lady who liked to speak in French and memorably once asked me on a holiday in France to address her as "*madame ma grandmère.*" She and Carina sometimes stayed in hotels in France or Switzerland for the summer and I used to join them there. They were lovely people; amusing, knowledgeable, caring and immensely dignified.

Caroline (Carina) Birman

Carina was born in Graz in Austria on the 1st of June 1895, the eldest daughter of a large family. The family were all blue eyed and Carina believed, without much knowledge of genetics, that although their Jewish 'desert pedigree' was untainted, the cool air in Austria had, over the centuries, effected this change!

Carina, however, had a great knowledge of the law. She studied in Paris and became Conseil Juridique in the Austrian Embassy in Paris from the mid 1920s to 1938 when the Anschluss closed the embassy down and all staff had to leave. She also had a link with the anti-Nazi, anti-communist fortnightly magazine *Das Tagebuch*, published at that time in Paris and founded in Germany by Stefan Grossman. Her friend, Grete Freund, was the financial manager there. It is possible that such writers as Franz Werfel and Stefan Zweig contributed to the magazine.

Carina was very resourceful and she facilitated an escape route for writers and artists who were being threatened with deportation by the Nazis. She invented a story that an arts festival was being organized in Mexico and persuaded the Mexican Ambassador that visas were needed for a group of people who had been invited to take part. He issued visas to everyone on her list.

My grandmother Sophie and Carina first met in 1927. From 1936 Sophie lived with Carina in Paris in Rue Lacrételle in the quinzième arrondisement. They finally settled together in the Gramercy area of New York.

Once in New York Carina took further law exams and became one of the few women admitted to the Supreme Court in Washington. In New York, where she worked as a solicitor, part of her legal work involved helping refugees with financial restitution from Germany. The Knights Templar, a religiously oriented Christian organization, wanted her as a member but she felt quite offended and indignantly turned them down because of what she saw as their history of anti-Semitism. She was not at all religious but was very conscious of her Jewishness. She wrote the account of her escape over the Pyrenees in 1975, after Sophie's death.

It was Carina who helped me revise for my Edinburgh University philosophy exams in a Swiss Hotel where I was staying one summer with her and Sophie. She cut through any confusion like a knife through butter; she had a laser mind. I appreciated her certainty and her complete clarity of vision.

Carina died in New York in 1996 at the age of nearly 101, twenty one years after Sophie, and her ashes are now buried alongside those of Sophie in a local New York Cemetery.

Franz and Alma Werfel

Franz Viktor Werfel was born in Prague, Bohemia (now the Czech Republic), on the 10th September 1890 as the first child of Albine and Rudolf Werfel, a prosperous glove factory owner. The Werfels were assimilated Jews, and young Franz was not raised in orthodoxy. Later in life, he learned Hebrew and studied the Talmud and the Bible in depth: an influence reflected in many of his works. Like his friends from Prague, Max Brod and Franz Kafka, Werfel never forgot his Jewish roots.

In 1929 Werfel and Alma Mahler-Gropius, the widow of the great composer Gustav Mahler, were married. Alma Mahler-Werfel, a composer in her own right and an artistic spirit, became the muse of his later productions. The couple lived in Vienna, but traveled extensively in Europe and the Middle East, including Israel. In 1933, in Vienna, Werfel wrote his novel *Die vierzig Tage des Musa Dagh (The Forty Days of Musa Dagh)*, about the Turkish massacre of the Armenians. (Hitler is quoted as saying just before the invasion of Poland "After all, who remembers the massacre of the Armenians?")

The Werfels remained in Vienna until Germany annexed Austria in 1938. At this point, they were forced to leave the country and fled to France where they lived first in Paris, then in Sanary-sur-Mer near Marseilles. When Germany invaded France, they attempted to flee to Spain and en route found refuge in Lourdes. Here Werfel made a vow to write a book about Bernadette Soubirous if they managed to escape the German troops. They crossed the Pyrenees on foot, traveled through Spain to Portugal and sailed to the United States where they arrived in October 1940. They settled in Beverly Hills, California, where Werfel spent the remainder of his life. He fulfilled his promise and wrote his bestselling novel *Das Lied von Bernadette (The Song of Bernadette)*, in 1941. He died in 1945.

Stefan Zweig

"Only the misfortune of exile can provide the in-depth understanding and the overview into the realities of the world" - Stefan Zweig

Born 1881, the son of a Jewish textile merchant Moritz Zweig and Ida Zweiss, the daughter of an Italian banker, Stefan Zweig was a sensitive and complicated personality. He was a humanist and student of philosophy and the history of literature in Vienna from 1900-1904, and it was there that he developed his ideals of peace, liberty of the individual and moral unity of the world.

Like most Jews he could not grasp that he would be banned and persecuted because of his Jewish origin. Zweig went into exile to England in 1936. Two years later he got a divorce from his wife Frederike and married his secretary Lotte Altmann.

He was a prolific writer whose books were burnt by the Nazis. One of his best known works *'Erasmus of Rotterdam'* was written in London and Bath from 1934-1940. In 1940, after a successful lecture tour in Brazil he settled there. Disillusioned and isolated, he and Lotte committed suicide together on 23 February 1942 in Petropolis near Rio de Janeiro. Brazil's populist dictator Getulio Vargas ordered the State to pay for their funeral.

Stefan's first wife Frederike, was mentioned in the memoir as having already left by a different route over the Pyrenees with her two daughters and their husbands, one of them carrying Shooshoo, her dog.

Lisa Fittko
[from her obituary published in The Times, 22 April 2005]

Lisa Fittko ran one of the most successful escape routes out of Nazi-occupied Europe.

Among the first to join her freedom trail across the Pyrenees was the Austrian writer Franz Werfel and his wife, Alma, who had previously

26

been married to the composer Gustav Mahler and the architect Walter Gropius.

Fittko herself had to turn back into Vichy France every time she reached the Spanish border because she was stateless and had no passport. She had grown up in Vienna and Berlin as Lisa Ekstein, daughter of a Hungarian businessman. Her involvement with the German Communist Party meant that she had to flee to Prague when the Nazis came to power in Berlin on January 30, 1933. There she married Hans Fittko.

A further escape to Paris led to her internment as an "enemy alien" once war began in 1939. She was detained in a women's camp in the Pyrenees when France collapsed in 1940 and the camp was dissolved.

She joined the Emergency Rescue Committee run by the American Quaker Varian Fry with the support of the American authorities and the exiled German writer Thomas Mann. With Hans she finally managed to escape to Cuba in 1941, and from there she reached the United States in 1948. She sought to catch up with a "normal life", first as a secretary, then as a librarian at the University of Chicago.

She did not return to her dramatic past until almost 40 years later, when she published her story *My Path over the Pyrenees* and enjoyed a late flowering as a lecturer and chat show guest.

Henny Gurland (née Schoenstedt)

The two people accompanying Benjamin to Port Bou were Henny Gurland and her son José aged 14. Until now the main evidence for Benjamin's suicide comes from a note, sent to Theodor Weisengrund Adorno, reconstituted and written on a postcard by Gurland in French.

Evidence suggests that Benjamin had written suicide notes in German and had given them to Gurland with an instruction to memorize and destroy them.

With her son, Gurland succeeded in escaping to the United States. In 1944 she married Erich Fromm. She died in 1952, after a long illness.

Walter Benjamin

The course of human history is a path of accumulating destruction which 'the angel' views with horror but from which he cannot turn away - (précis from 'Theses on the Philosophy of History' in Walter Benjamin's *Illuminations* in which he describes Paul Klee's picture Angelus Novus).

Few 20th century thinkers have proved as influential as Walter Benjamin. One of the first serious writers about film and photography, Benjamin's thought and philosophical reflections have had a major impact on theorists in literature, philosophy, historical studies and theories in the contemporary arts.

Walter Benjamin was born in 1892 to a prosperous Jewish family in Berlin. He became a student of philosophy and worked as a cultural and literary critic. He wrote many books and essays, inspired by the Marxism of his friend Bertold Brecht, the Jewish mysticism of Gershom Scholem and the critical theory of Adorno. Benjamin left Germany and went to Paris when the Nazis came into power in 1933, because, as he described it "One could no longer breathe the air in Germany." Paris was an inspiration for him and during that period he wrote some of his most influential essays and articles, including 'The Arcades Project' and the 'The Work of Art in the Age of Mechanical Reproduction' which is much admired as a prophetic work and has great relevance today.

In 1915 Benjamin married the beautiful and musically talented translator, writer and journalist Dora Pollack (Kellner). They had a son, Stefan Raphael, in 1918. The couple later divorced in 1930 but Dora remained very supportive. She went to England with Stefan. Dora tried to persuade her ex-husband to leave Paris and also to take refuge in England but he preferred to remain in situ until the occupying German army forced him to flee over the Pyrenees. The Port Bou register of deaths lists him as dying at 10 p.m. on September 26th 1940.

Notes on 'Passages', the monument to Walter Benjamin at Port Bou.

(from *Walter Benjamin A Biography*, Momme Brodersen, London, 1996).

In October 1940 the philosopher Hannah Arendt passed through Port Bou and tried without success to find the grave of her friend Walter Benjamin. She described her visit to Gershom Scholem in Israel: 'The cemetery looks out over a small bay directly on the Mediterranean. Its terraces are hewn out of stone and coffins are also put in these stone walls. This is one of the most fantastic and beautiful places I have ever seen.' Until 1979, when a small plaque was erected in the cemetery there was no public commemoration of Benjamin in Port Bou, although it seems that many in the town remembered the fate of this German refugee, had made him into a kind of local symbol for all of the other forgotten victims of fascism.

In 1990, commissioned by the Arbeitskreis Selbständiger Kultur-institute (ASKI) in Bonn on behalf of the German government, the Israeli artist Dani Karavan began planning a large-scale monument in Port Bou. Karavan was already renowned for his remarkable monumental work in Israel and elsewhere: it included a memorial for victims of the Holocaust at the Weizmann Institute at Rehovot, the 'Kikar Levana-White Square' environment in Tel Aviv, and an installation at the 1976 Venice Biennale dedicated to peace between the Arabs and Israelis, 'Olive Trees should be our Borders'.

The Port Bou monument 'Passages' was inaugurated in May 1994. Its centrepiece is a flight of 70 narrow steps cut into the cliff at the seaward side of the cemetery, running down at an angle of 30° through rusty iron walls to a dizzying dead-end overlooking the rocks and sea below. A glass screen terminates the passage; compelled to retrace their steps, visitors turn to face the cemetery, and before emerging from the tunnel are confronted by a wall of undressed stone, set in the axial extension of the corridor into a rock-face surrounding the cemetery forecourt. The sea, the cemetery: no way out.

Banyuls-sur-Mer

MEDITERRANEAN

0   kilometres   1

FRANCE

PYRENEES

SPAIN

Port Bou

The terrain of the escape from Banyuls to Port Bou, 1940

Carina Birman in New York, 1972

Carina Birman, Kathy Duggan and Sophie Lippmann in Klosters, Switzerland, in the early 1970

Sophie Lippmann's house in Gabitzstrasse in Breslau

Sophie Lippmann, with her daughter Barbara, circa 1916

At the customs house in Port Bou

Kathy Duggan outside the former Fonda de Francia to which the
refugees, including her grandmother Sophie Lippmann,
were directed and where Walter Benjamin died.

A view of Port Bou from the mountains

Kathy Duggan on the French/Spanish border at the foot of the Pyrenees; the end of the escape r

A plaque near Walter Benjamin's funeral monument in Port Bou

A picture of Walter Benjamin on the wall of the town museum in Port Bou

Schwerer ist es, das Gedächtnis der Namenlosen zu ehren als das der Berühmten.
Dem Gedächtnis der Namenlosen ist die historische Konstruktion geweiht.
Walter Benjamin. G.S. I, 1241

Inscription in German on the glass wall at the end of the memorial built by Karavan:
'*It is more difficult to honour the memory of the nameless than of the well-known. Historical construction is dedicated to the memory of the nameless.*' Walter Benjamin, *On the Concept of History.*

Facing page:
Port Bou cemetery on the Mediterranean where Walter Benjamin was buried under the name Benj
Walter following a Catholic rite

Walter Benjamin's grave in the Port Bou cemetery. The inscription, from Benjamin's own works, re "There is never a cultural document without at the same time it being a document of barbarism."